# ALL THE PAINTINGS OF
# **BOTTICELLI**

## Part 3

### *VOLUME TWENTY-SEVEN*
*in the*
*Complete Library of World Art*

*The Complete Library of World Art*

# ALL THE PAINTINGS

# OF **BOTTICELLI**

## Part 3 (1485–1510)

*Text by* ROBERTO SALVINI

*Translated from the Italian by*
JOHN GRILLENZONI

HAWTHORN BOOKS, INC.
*Publishers* · *New York*

*Printed and bound in Great Britain by Jarrold & Sons Ltd., Norwich*

# CONTENTS

# ALL THE PAINTINGS OF
## BOTTICELLI

# SANDRO BOTTICELLI

## *Life and Work*

BOTTICELLI'S stay in Rome, between 1481 and 1482, was of great importance in the development of his art. Although the portraits of the popes and the three great biblical cycles he painted in the Sistine Chapel may, in themselves, be of lesser importance, they nevertheless stimulated his imagination. His stay in Rome not only made him more aware of the power of classical art (to which his humanism already disposed him), but he benefited from the contact he made with Perugino and Signorelli. Most important of all, however, was the fact that he was now compelled to resolve the problems of the monumental representation of complex symbolical and allegorical stories, so that they would be meaningful even to the illiterate.

Without denying his essential style—which lay in the projection of reality by means of detached, idealized images —he perfected the natural qualities of those images to the point where he achieved a fine balance between realism and idealism. This is apparent both from the more fully realized parts of the frescoes, and the *Pallas and the Centaur* (Part 2, plate 113). This, in a certain sense, is the most classic moment of Botticelli's art, whether in a mythological subject like the *Pallas* (everything indicated he painted this after he left Rome), or in a religious one like the famous *tondo*, the *Madonna of the Magnificat* (plate 1). A clear indication of the revival of this naturalism is the fact that the same theme he had treated earlier in the *Raczinsky Tondo* in Berlin (plate 63, Part 1) is renewed here with a reminiscence of Fra Filippo, a characteristic part of Sandro's youthful work. The suggestion of a quiet plastic rhythm we perceive in Lippi's painting, so far away in time, returns in the linear rendering of the turning volumes. The easy curves of the figures' outlines fit nicely into the round frame, and the line proceeds perhaps too flowingly. But the line becomes one with the modulation of the volumes and their slow turning, accentuated by the slight dissymmetry of the two points where the Virgin's hand touches the angels, and where the two angels hold the crown. The landscape in the background is only suggested: the line of the twisting river and the rolling hills repeats the musical line of the group, until the echo fades in the far distance. Thus the natural beauty of the figures and the "psychology" of souls caught up in a moment of adoration are fully invoked. Unfortunately earlier retouching has obscured much of the detail.

Another painting of the same period, the *Madonna of the Book* in Milan (plate 5), seems to render the grace of the *Madonna of the Magnificat* in a more contained way. Free of retouching, it helps us imagine what the Uffizi *Madonna* must have been like. This is particularly true of the limpid color, enamel-like but suffused and pale, which contributes no less than the other elements to the balance between naturalism and ideal abstraction which became the new ground on which Botticelli played subtle variations.

The *Mars and Venus* in London (plate 8) exemplifies this balance between nature and idea, expressed by the close pairing of the line and the arrangement of the volumes, the planimetric development and the spatial "consistency" of the composition. The effect might lead us to suppose mistakenly, as, for instance, Argan has done recently, that the work is a youthful one. It has already been noted that the reclining figures facing front (like the fauns playing with the god's lance, plate 10) come from a late-Roman sarcophagus in the Vatican Museum (Tietze-Conrat). And certainly the isocephalism of the figures, reclining in the foreground against the thick foliage of the wood and the extended greenish sea, is a classical motif. This allusion to the ancient world does not however mean mere imitation but becomes part of the work itself, as we have already seen in the *Primavera* (Part 2, plates 64–65) and *Pallas and the Centaur*. The allusion serves to clothe reality with myth. Furthermore, here the formal completeness suggested by classic models finds response in the way the volume has been keyed to the line—a particularly evident stylistic fact in this period in the artist's development. And even the space does not exist as something to be filled, like a predetermined box in perspective waiting to be packed with forms, but rather emerges, real and unreal, from the unifying play of line and volume. Line governs the easy arrangement of planes in the bodies of the two gods, which is emphasized by the rhythm of the turning volumes of the fauns as they continue the melody of the composition and enclose the space. The balanced relation of the masses and the isometry of the heads are determining elements in that free rhythm.

Closely related to this painting, because of the similarity to the figure of Venus, are the five portraits of a girl, in which past criticism has tried to see the lovely Simonetta Cattaneo (Part 4, plates 127–130a). The portraits are too much alike not to be considered workshop copies. And the style shows that they were executed too late to be portraits of Giuliano de' Medici's beloved, who died very young in 1476. Although of good quality, not one of them is worthy of Botticelli. Indeed, only the copy formerly in Munich (plate 129a) admits the possibility of his having painted parts. Botticelli's capacities as a portrait painter are really revealed in the *Portrait of a Youth* in London (plate 7). This splendid painting has less linear tension, less visible plasticity than the more naturalistic portraits which form the frescoes in the Sistine Chapel, but is rich in its apparent simplicity, in the coherence of the modulated form and line. The youth seems to linger between actuality and the evocation of a pure image of spiritual, melancholy beauty.

During this highpoint in Botticelli's creativity, he painted the *Birth of Venus*, in a way, the most classic of his works. The subject itself is obviously classical, but it is not merely an ideal reconstruction of the famous painting by Apelles. There is a Grecian quality about the painting—the figure of the goddess is like a marble statue brought to life only by Zephyr's warm breath, a startling allusion to the "Aphrodite Anadiomenes" of the Greeks, as she was imagined in Poliziano's poetry. Botticelli could have learned of her through the poet or through the classical sources he was near in Rome. If the artist had caught the image, in the *Judith* and in the *Primavera*, at the moment when movement becomes stasis, here, on the contrary, the figure of Venus seems caught at the moment when her lifelessness quickens into life. But the image here is—again—suspended in a sad perplexity against a mythical, timeless horizon.

The classical spirit of the subject and the remarkable recreation of mythic tone are not weakened, as Gombrich has perceptively noted, by the fact that the composition echoes the traditional iconographic presentation of the "Baptism of Christ". As Argan points out: it only shows that "the rendering has an essentially spiritual and not sensual character," and, he goes on, "this beautiful woman's body which . . . sublimates the physical with its diaphanous forms and pure lines is a challenge, an intellectual challenge, thrown to sensuality." It also shows that a religious spirit and a profound moral consciousness pervade the mythological elements with the result that they naturally embody the allegorical meanings derived from Ficino's Neo-Platonism. And this transformation is dual; the sense of myth and the feeling for an image invoked from a legendary past invest the sacred subject. The complex and, in a certain sense, ambivalent spiritual attitude the artist assumes, which a more recent tradition credits to the "sophisticated" Vasari, was part of the spiritual and cultural climate in which we find not only Poliziano's serene poetry but also the tormented speculative efforts of a Pico della Mirandola and of a Ficino to reconcile reason and faith, the classic and the Christian worlds, through Platonic philosophy.

But the "content" is meaningful from the point of view of art only insofar as it finds expression in the spontaneous coherence of the artist's idiom. To analyze it, perhaps we should begin with his sense of space which, if rightly interpreted, can furnish a key to understanding the master's style in this crucial phase. The quiet expanse of the green water, in which the dominant color of the fabulous shores seems reflected, does not exclude a sense of spaciousness; the horizon is just perceptibly broken by the tongues of land which stretch to the sea. This kind of space does not have any vigorous perspective, and the same graduated licks of land, by suggesting with their flexible outlines a rather undulating line, seem to extend into unreal distances the frenetic line of the embroidered cloak Hora stretches toward the naked Venus. By such relationships among the lines even the horizon loses significant spatial meaning. The expanse of sea and sky can easily serve as a plane of reference for the undulating line of the group, without, on the other hand, assuming the hermetic smoothness of a neutral ground. Space finally becomes the backdrop for the figures, while by an analogous process the development of the line becomes one with the rhythmic rotation of the volumes. A rather singular style results, in which the line dominates the composition without thereby becoming a mere arabesque, as we observed in the *Primavera*. That is, neither volume nor space are overwhelmed, but are rather included in the line's play, which is accompanied by modulated color—pale tints that glow. This perfect unity of volume and line appears especially in the marvelous figures of the Zephyrs (plate 14), whose entwined bodies are made to seem less monstrous by their very transparency despite the three legs that seem to unfold from one body. The outline which defines them against the still chromatic expanse of water and sky contributes to the effect, but more importantly perhaps, the spinning lines of the draperies which encircle like rounding volumes the arm and abdomen of one Wind and the breast of his companion.

In the figure of Venus, the turns of the line are more concentrated. Curves are emphasized by repetition: the turn of the right leg and then of the left arm, and from there the inflection of the neck and the flow of her hair. The figure is more clearly cut off from the plane, and the relationship between them more direct. But the sinuous curve of her left side corresponds to the billowing mantle, and thus a continuity is established with the figure of Hora, which is a more complex play of forms and lines (plate 17).

Here again Botticelli's achievement is reconfirmed—his capacity to reach the heights of a sensuous naturalism and, at the same time, a pure spirituality. The *Birth of Venus* may be taken as the symbol and exemplar of his art, by this singular fusion of linear, spatial and volumetric values, and by the natural color which he idealizes with a shimmering transparency. The hidden Neo-Platonic meaning of the allegory seems plausible by the method of the painting which relates content with form. The painting celebrates, surely, the ideal of beauty which is born of the union between spirit and matter, between idea and nature. This ideal of cosmic harmony, we should note at once, does not conceal a new anxiety. The clear signs of dissymmetry among so much symmetry threaten the stability of the composition, and Venus's lines have a ductile quality which suggest languor, while the lines of the Winds are too complex and strained. There is an almost oriental lightness in the slow raining of flowers on the water, and the same quality persists in the attenuated circumflexes of the waves. The result betrays a melancholy and an excess of feeling which streak the crystalline harmony of the whole.

Almost forty, Botticelli painted the *Birth of Venus* not only as the highpoint of his art, but also as a presage of future developments which would turn out to be much more tormented.

In 1485, the year in which he painted the altarpiece for Santo Spirito, Botticelli began a new phase in his art. In the *Madonna and Child with SS John the Baptist and John the Evangelist*, the style is certainly related to the *Birth of Venus*. The composition of the triptych was presaged in the Uffizi canvas. The Virgin's hand reaching for her breast, like Venus's hand, seems to play an arpeggio. I would even say that the outlines of the Madonna resemble Venus's. But here also arise the differences between the two works. The rather melodic line we saw in the *Birth of Venus*, which touches upon the melancholy becomes more tense in the figure of the Virgin. It undergoes sudden interruptions and turns in the folds of her clothing. If the landscape in the *Venus*, the water, sky and plants, took on an air of fantasy from the melodious play of the figures, here the charming shrubbery (beyond which we can just make out a bluish sky) is a naturalistic metaphor for the traditional divisions—thrones and niches— of a triptych. Thus by paralleling the function of the background to a traditional medieval scheme, the artist could go beyond the mere spiritualization of nature into fable. Nature here becomes symbol. The meanings which Christianity endows the olive, the palm and the lily are not imposed on the painting, but become part of its expression. We have a clear analogy here, by this mythologizing, with the artist's previous paintings in which the allusions to the ancient world created the sense of classicism. Here the allusion to archaic composition, and the rendering of traditional typology, intensify the religiosity of the work without imitating religious works *per se*. The stasis of the images is iconic; the harsh linear rendering isolates them in a sorrowful, meditative silence. The accent has been displaced toward a poetic transfiguration of religious emotions, but we do not attribute the superior reality of these figures just to this, but rather because they too seem to evoke, with their allusions, a distant past, a profound atavistic memory.

The aspiration toward an ideal beauty that was tinged with nostalgia, a beauty that arises from perfect union of matter and spirit, is being replaced by an aspiration toward a different kind of beauty. No less nostalgic, this beauty arises from the moment when spirit possesses the body and animates it with the urge to adoration. From this point on, and not by chance, Botticelli's subjects would be sacred ones, except for some rare portraits.

In the *Madonna of the Pomegranate* (1487), the theme of the *tondo* is resolved differently from the *Madonna of the Magnificat* (plate 1). The angels close in an arch over the Virgin, the rhythm of the heads is discordant, the Virgin's figure pyramids upwards and creates a sense of anxious aspiration despite the tranquility of the whole. Of course, not everything seems resolved in the painting. The artist is too concerned with attracting the viewer by the insistent stares of his subjects; he is too careful with the attractive poses of the figures to be caught up in the implications of line and color. The musicality of the composition is present, but not to an absolute degree of coherence. It is something more like a dirge accompanying repetitious words.

The urgency of his new spiritual interests cause a moment of crisis. Even if in the *Madonna* in Berlin (plate 20), he had found a perfect expression for them, sometimes, and especially in this case, the synthesis between form and content is not so complete. A feeling of extenuating and almost sick melancholy, and a tendency to overload the image with moral meanings sometimes fail to achieve a desirable end. We mean this to be understood—as a critical judgment—with some care, because no work by Botticelli completely lacks moments of real art. A lapse into a superficial description of languor occurs, for instance, as in the *Portrait of a Youth* in Washington (plate 24), despite the beauty of the hand and the live modeling of the jacket. On the other hand, his control is greater in other works, as in the *Madonna* in Edinburgh (plate 28), which is so compact and intimate—except for some collaborators' hastiness—because of the precise line.

This crisis is not overcome even in the *St Barnabas Altarpiece* (plate 29). Indeed, the effort to achieve a monumental and ritual altarpiece—an effort which is betrayed besides by the fact that Botticelli was unwilling to accept any suggestions from Filippino—weighs on this work. The monumental plan, the rather arid limits of the perspective, seem alien to the master's spirit. The figures themselves have a kind of plastic gravity which is consonant with the genre, but not with Botticelli's imagination. The weaving of the lines becomes tenser, more energetic and recalls in a more complicated and perhaps painful way the themes from Pollaiuolo he had imitated as a young artist. Note the thinness of the Virgin and Child (plate 30) or the vibrancy of St Michael the Archangel in his shining armor. The figure and head of St John the Baptist (plate 32) form one of Botticelli's more intense masterpieces. Here the feeling of suffering mankind, of a tormented ascetic spirit, arises from the broken and springing lines and from the hammered and contorted planes which make up the figure. In the smaller panels of the predella, we hardly notice the stiffness of some of the work, done by collaborators, for the sheer imaginativeness and spontaneity of the scenes. In the *Vision of St Augustine* (plate 34), in the *Pietà* (plate 35) and in the *Salome* (plate 36), a new sense of unrelieved solitude appears in the bare backgrounds. Space becomes unreal because of its undefined and unrelated breadth. A new element is present in the miraculous participation of nature in the drama of the *Pietà*. The thin plants behind Christ flicker like the small figures which recapitulate the Passion in the background. Against these undefined spaces, as in the dark wall in the *Extraction of St Ignatius's Heart*, we find rare figures (plate 37) defined with an unusual density of color.

I consider the *Annunciation* in the Uffizi Gallery (plate 38) to be Botticelli's own work, and perfectly realized, despite the opinion of several scholars. Documents indicate that the painting was done in 1489 or between 1489 and 1490, for the church in Cestello. Once we overcome the first, somewhat unpleasant, impression we have of the scorched colors and the aridity (a product of the usury of the times) the painting emerges in its positive values. How striking is the angel impelled by the mysterious mission he has been given toward the Virgin, as she sways toward him like a reed. The tumult of his billowing robes is brought back to unity by the curve of the veils, which in turn are reinforced in their dynamic function by the wings. A current of spiritual energy is transmitted from the angel's arm upwards to the Virgin whose body arches expectantly. The complex plotting of lines underscores the pathos of the scene of the two figures on the same plane. But the fact that they are on the same plane does not lessen the perspective clarity of the room, since the accent does not fall on the geometry of the space, but rather—as an effective counterpoint—on the movement toward the open country beyond the window. Space here is conceived not as the scene of the action, but as a romantic flight. And, in fact, the landscape is filled (plate 39) with walls, towers and Gothic castles. Flemish motifs reflect Botticelli's taste for the exotic and add what little of the fabulous a distant land can evoke. But we cannot extend the meaning of these motifs in Botticelli's art to claim he was trying to approach Flemish painting, as we could and do say for a Filippino, a Ghirlandaio or a Lorenzo di Credi. There is nothing here of the quiet awe for the oneness of man and nature as in the Flemish masters, or even the curiosity for the minor aspects of reality as we find in the superficial "Flemishness" of some Florentines. Botticelli fantasizes on a line which unfolds easily and gently behind the lilies. He rejected Flemish naturalism precisely because it left such little room for his fantasy . . . and his spirit.

A quick, barely drawn psychological comment on the pathos of the figures is the landscape in the *Coronation of the Virgin* (plate 42), which Botticelli painted in this period for St Mark's. Leonardo, as we know, did not like Sandro's landscapes. For Leonardo, nature was an object of intense research; to draw a plant or a rock meant to recreate the object in its truest reality, in the innate reason for its existence (and Leonardo's rocks bear witness to his geological inquiries; his plants and flowers reflect a true sense of their growth). But for Botticelli, nature was simply a means at times of completing a rhythm, as if to empty some of the sentiment he had packed into his figures.

Here, for instance, the landscape suggests only an indefinite spatial vastness which is quickly absorbed by the vertical development of the composition. What little shows through of the harsh lines is psychologically consonant with the indestructible rock-like figures of the saints. Apparently Botticelli tried to find a plastic "robustness" again, as he had tried in the *St Barnabas Altarpiece* (plate 29). But here the planes are distended, separated by a thick chromatic substance, and divided unexpectedly by the drawn-out lines of the edges and the draperies. We can not deny the excessive illustrative elements, excessive, that is, with respect to the painting's capacity to absorb them; in other words, conventionality. Nonetheless, as a whole, the figures succeed in interpreting the moral gravity of the subject. Their stability, on the other hand, accentuates the contrast with the almost dionysiac dance around the divine group (plates 44–45). The line which encloses the Virgin and God in the pointed lunette is extremely effective; the tension is released only by the frenetic dance.

"The chain of dancers rises on the right with a quick and festive rhythm, descends in a whirl on the left, and between the two ends of the eclipse tends almost to snap in order to regain its impetus. . . . Hand passes on to hand the impulse of the flight, the rhythm of the dance. The lines of the bodies, now taut in space, now loosened, carried along by the wind or broken by the beat of the dance: profiles pitched against the impetus or relaxed in the languor of the ecstasy, their hair falling in loose streams moved by the bacchic currents mark different times in cadence with the movement . . ." (A. Venturi).

Everything is resolved in the line's impetuous play as now it tenses, then relaxes, or pauses to describe with a slow curve the spiritual grace of a curly head, or races along with the leaping bodies. This, then, is not a real world, but one which arises from the artist's imagination as the embodiment of his religious enthusiasm, just as earlier his worlds embodied a sad nostalgia for more serene and classical images.

There is this new touch in the very delicate predella. We sense the change in the silence which seems to pervade the two figures in the *Annunciation* (plate 47a), and also in *St John on Patmos* (plate 46a) where the harsh lines of the rocks are repeated in the angular draping of the figure. Everywhere, as if to confirm the moral intent, stretches a barren solitude. In contrast, other artists during this period, with Ghirlandaio at their head, would fill landscapes and interiors scrupulously. Compare the firm synthesis Botticelli achieves in the blacksmith's shop in the *Miracles of St Eligius* (plate 48), in the cave in *St Jerome* (plate 47b) or the studio in *St Augustine* (plate 46b). The solitude brings out the meaning, rather more contemplative than dramatic; these are not stories, but presentations of images—of the events and persons portrayed. The solitude breathes in the soft and luminous light of some areas, and in others, in the vivid, archaically precious tones.

There is a spiritual solitude which attracts us to lesser paintings intended for pious purposes, like the *Madonna* in Dresden (plate 52) or like the *Madonna* in Washington (plate 60). On the other hand, a heroic austerity recalling the saints in the *Coronation of the Virgin* relives in the *Portrait of*

*Marullus* (plate 62) and especially in the one of *Lorenzano* (plate 61). The *Portrait of Lorenzano*, in fact, gives us an idea of how the saints in the *St Mark Altarpiece* might have appeared if some stubborn insistence had not blurred the expressive clarity of the painting. The figure is heavy, almost massive in its plastic fullness, but distended also along the plane and compressed there, so that rather than settling in a space related to the viewer, it seems to emerge from an indefinite depth. The figure takes form from the darkness into the light, as if evoked magically. The man is strongly defined in his individuality, both physical and psychological. Even perhaps absolute and unreal, he admonishes us about the religious austerity of knowledge and thought.

We are certain now that these works reveal—the portraits no less than the church paintings—that Botticelli became a proselyte of the Christian faith. He had always been religious, because he had moved toward a Platonic, spiritual beauty. In these later paintings, his feeling is expressed by his interpretation of religion as a heroic moral commitment, and somewhat as a mystical experience. Thus he shows affinities with Savonarola much before he was actually to come under the friar's influence, along with the crowds who went to hear him preach around 1490.

And yet, moments of lighter, subtler emotion, more intimate and less portentous intonations can occasionally be seen, as in the *Madonna of the Pavilion* in the Ambrosiana (plate 54). Here we see some reminders of the dance in the *Coronation of the Virgin*, but the spirit is more modulated, the tone more sensitive, the line less impetuous. This calmer spirit enhances the *Annunciation* formerly in the Lehman Collection (plate 56). The perspective is neatly divided and serves to isolate the two figures by creating around them a spatial "cup" which induces a great stillness.

The irregular return, in this period just after 1490, to compositions in definite perspective should not be interpreted to mean a return to naturalism, but interpreted in the light of his increasing detachment from the world. The *St Augustine* (plate 59) in the Uffizi Gallery, for example, shows a figure compressed by the very sharp and interrupted lines into a space which can only be the moral place for the saint's faith and his thoughts. The objects and the lucidity of the colors react precisely to this image of internality.

In the meantime, Botticelli was moved by the persuasive preaching of Savonarola and meditated more deeply on the mystery of the sacrifice, as we see in the *Lamentation* in Munich (plate 65) and the one in Milan (plate 66). In these two paintings, the palpable reality of the figures is transformed into pure images and achieves the level of sacred symbol by means of the unreality of the rhythm which binds and tightens the figures in a compelling composition. In the first *Lamentation* (plate 65), the figures gather against the dark background of the rock cave and bend in a grieving arch over the dead body. But the version in the Poldi-Pezzoli Museum (plate 66) is more intense, more expressive: the broken rhythm of lines is similar but orders itself vertically in a hammered graduation of masses enclosed by the two inclining Marys. Only Michelangelo, Argan writes, "will understand the value of such a composition, which avoids the crudeness of drama and the abstraction of idea at the same time, since reality is enclosed, as a tragic presence, in the Idea."

In the unfinished *Adoration* (plate 70) in the Uffizi, it seems almost as if a sudden gust of wind, springing from between the rocks, thrusts everyone toward the Holy Family. But in the endless repetition of the same arching, upward movement that never joins in a complete figure, the intense drama of the scene is freed from mere history and is translated into a moving allegory, the foreboding of grief and redemption. And, dissimilar as the paintings may appear, the same principle holds in the *Communion of St Jerome* (plate 69), where the composition centers in the arch formed by the communicant and the friar. The triangular movement created by the roof draws our attention to the three emblematic palm branches. The spiritual intensity of the sacrament is revealed directly beneath, with a rhythm of tightly knit lines and gem-like colors.

Botticelli's usual tendency to project nature and history into myth and allegory finds an unusual opportunity in these same years. Around 1490 presumably, Lorenzo di Pierfrancesco de' Medici asked him to prepare some illustrations for Dante's *Divine Comedy*. We can believe he accepted the charge willingly, even if he had not suggested it himself. Vasari tells us that Botticelli had spent some time studying the great poem. Rather than approaching the poem directly, he tried to distill the meaning as it was contained in key episodes. As if he realized that his drawings could never capture the full import of the lines, he commented with his art on the poet's itinerary through the fantastic moral world of the *Comedy*, presenting the images as they appear to the pilgrim, in all their horror or glory.

In illustrating each canto, he sought a figurative unity beyond any conventional perspective, in a "kind of view from above where the figures seem flattened, and at times even flattened out into the carpet . . ." (Bertini). Frequently, therefore, we have a sense of the marvelous, realized through the lyric mode of illustrations like the one for Canto IX of the *Inferno* (plate 75), with the gate to the city of Dis and the "mud people" of the Styx. The daring "cut" of the composition, with its wide curves, succeeds in embracing the scattered groups in a contained rhythm. The general atmosphere of fable is made more immediate and more moving by the wide arc of the figures of the wrathful in the swamp.

In the beautiful representation of the forest of the suicides (*Inferno*, Canto XIII; plate 76), the description contained in a verse ("not green leaves but of a dark color/not straight branches, but knotty and twisted/there were no apples, but only poison twigs") becomes the dominant theme of the whole drawing. The thorny branches weave across the sheet, suggesting by their sharp linearity the immense space involved and the temporal progress of the two poets. In the bowge of the counterfeiters (*Inferno*, Canto XXIX; plate 78) the drawing unfolds through both wide and tight curves, with interruptions and renewals, following a tiring rhythm that echoes the now broken now prolonged beat of certain verses. But the drawing lacks Dante's characterization and his realism (thus the lepers Griffolino and Capocchio are pitiful as they lean back to back, while Dante's description is bitter: "just as in cooking we lean pot against pot").

Therefore, it is the visual element in Dante's poetry that Botticelli takes up and transforms into his own images. His capacity to illustrate the original text with drawings that have merit of their own, even if they are not "total" expressions, can best be seen in the *Purgatorio* sequence. Here the drawing at times is so fine as not to require a distinct composition to achieve unity. The rendering of details is frequently as expressive as the rendering of groups, as in the group of the invidious (the folio related to Canto XV) where we see one enclosed by an arching movement and realized with a simplicity that can only be found again in the *Derelitta*. Or in the group of dancing angels which illustrate Canto XXXI, we find a very light line enlivening their movement which recalls the angelic choir in the *Coronation* in the Uffizi (plate 42).

The most poetic moments can be found in the illustrations of the earthly paradise in the last cantos of *Purgatorio*, and in the rarefied compositions of the third canticle. Except when some theological subtlety or some impalpable vision was difficult to render figuratively, Botticelli translated the luminous evanescence of Dante's *Paradiso* with the deftest touches and an extraordinary fluidity of rhythms. The drawing moves toward a new melodic unity through the circling of the groups that compose it. Representative of the whole sequence is the astonishing illustration for Canto I (plate 83), where "two light, silvery figures take to flight drawn one by the other, from the ethereal wood of saplings toward the . . . prime mover: a subtle combination of opposing movement (the figures and the trees), and of the crosscurrents of April which blow quickly, without weighing on the flowers" (A. Venturi). To better judge the originality which Botticelli showed in illustrating Dante, one need only remember the verse that provides the theme for this drawing: "Beatrice tutta nell'eterne rote/fissa con gli occhi stava; ed io in lei/le luci fissi di lassù remote" (Beatrice stood with her eyes fixed on the eternal spheres, and I saw in her the remote lights from above). The harmonious vision of the turning of the celestial spheres is translated in the drawing into an idyllic image. The ellipse of the river becomes symbolic of the idea of the circle implied by Dante's "eternal spheres." While the poet himself has become immersed in the heavens and has forgotten the world and the Garden of Eden, the drawing retains the memory, spiritual and moving, of the freshest and most idyllic nature.

The religious feeling, the profound moral aspiration which animate the illustrations from Dante are equally present in the paintings which were executed presumably around 1495 and shortly after. Among these, the most important and best known is the panel in the Uffizi with the allegorical figure of *Calumny* (plates 92–93). An unreal golden tonality infuses the sharply perspective space, which is made sumptuous by the rich gilt decoration and imposing by the three immense arches opening onto the quiet sea. But in this dream world decorated with figures from both classical myths and Christianity, reminders of pagan virtues and Christian saintliness, a storm has been let loose. Between the figures to the left of the judge and the first figure in the group of Calumny, which correspond inversely as in a mirror, there is a whirling of lines culminating in the repeated tension of Hate's and the judge's outstretched arms. The lines are tense and angular and break everywhere, as in the harsh figure of the naked victim, in the pointed corners of Penitence's robes, in the springing lines and unrest of Truth, while the statues themselves stand uneasily in their niches. Argan calls our attention to the continuous line of the central group; the episode enacted here of a victim dragged in by Calumny to spite Truth is not felt as a single instance, but rather as an event which will be forever repeated in that rich courtroom which symbolizes the ancient world. The symbol can be felt, moreover, not merely as belonging to a single age, but as the "distant kingdom of ideas, where the profound causes of human behavior lie." Thus implicit in this allegory is the recognition of the limits of ancient wisdom—or human wisdom—which cannot attain justice, since it was not enlightened by revelation or by grace.

The beautiful drawing in Darmstadt (plate 99) showing the despair of the faithless who have been excluded from the benefits that resulted from the descent of the Holy Ghost, and the *Derelitta* (if it can be interpreted as *Virtue Abandoned* or *lost Truth*) are evidence that Botticelli had these concepts in mind during this period. In any case, even if such an ingenious interpretation cannot be said to be proved, it is certain that unrest and anxiety, an impulse, as it were, toward purification, are poetically expressed by the *Calumny*. An analogous emotion pervades the famous and much discussed small painting entitled the *Derelitta* (the abandoned) however the subject may be interpreted. Tension is embodied in the curving figure, somewhat like the bent figures in the illustration for Canto XV of the *Purgatorio*. While the line is defined in the harsh segments of the white robe, echoed by the architectonic space and the steps, the scattered robes re-emphasize the anxiety.

The presence of a certain moral austerity and religious aspiration in the paintings of this period should not be interpreted, as is frequently done, as the effects of a conversion brought about under Savonarola's influence alone. Not only because, if it is said, the tendency develops gradually, and began even before the fiery Dominican began to preach with telling results in Florence, but also because Botticelli's temperament revealed itself in his early paintings as directed toward potentially religious contemplation. Even the paintings with mythological themes and apparent pagan inspiration are not in real contrast to Christian spirituality. Rather, they derive to a great extent from the neo-Platonic thinkers who tried to reconcile reason and faith, classical naturalism and Christian spiritualism. This is not to deny completely what Vasari says of Botticelli's participation in Savonarola's movement, or to deny that Savonarola's power and his tragic end contributed toward reinforcing Botticelli's latent tendencies which emerge, around 1500, as a real kind of mysticism.

The documents, and a large number of autograph and

*bottega* paintings disprove Vasari's claim that the artist was an adherent of Savonarola's "sect" and that having abandoned painting, he had nothing to live on, and his life became desperate. On the other hand, Botticelli certainly did not live apart from the religious tumult of the time. We know that his brother Simone was an ardent follower of Savonarola, and Sandro, who had never married, lived with him. Furthermore, it appears that Botticelli's relations with his principal Medici benefactor, Lorenzo di Pierfrancesco, flagged or came to an end, from what we can gather from the fact that the artist discontinued the illustrations of Dante and from the silence of the documents, just at the time when Lorenzo and his brother, who had both supported the Dominican friar, turned against him and helped bring about his end. If we relate his conversation with Doffo Spini, cited in his brother's diary, in which Sandro asks Spini what sins Savonarola had committed to deserve "such a vile death," with the epigraph in the *Mystic Nativity* in London (plate 114), we find it difficult to understand the doubts of several even recent scholars about Botticelli's sensitivity to those events. We can dismiss the possibility of his being an active partisan or mourner, but his work confirms that he suffered through the violent events of those days.

In 1499, just a year after Savonarola had been burned, Botticelli painted the panels—the *Tragedy of Virginia* (plate 102) and the *Tragedy of Lucretia* (plate 103) which are among his most passionate and melancholy compositions. The wide and deep space of the composition does not attempt any kind of compactness, nor is there a constant rhythm among the groups who unite and separate along the horizontal plane of the foreground and the architectonic structure shoved into the background. Rather we have the impression of a vacuum that acts like a suction, drawing in or expelling the groups of small figures. In the *Tragedy of Virginia*, the divergence of the two lines of pilasters which move outwards right to the upper part of the frame seems to impel the centrifugal movement of the groups, in turn counteracted by the yawning cavity of the apse in the center of the composition. The line acts as a whirlwind, dominating the entire composition with a continuous and exhausting play of tensions and distensions. A stiffening of some outlines gives way to an upward spiraling or flame-like movement of some forms. This agitation, a continuing energy without pause or conclusion, mitigates the purely historical character of both paintings, and projects them into an ideal world beyond time. The event, like a myth, is imbued with allegorical meaning which can, at any moment, be reinvoked by the consciousness. The lucidity of the color accentuates the unreality and heightens the effect of a vision which the paintings create.

We come to the *Mystic Nativity*, without pausing as we should to comment on other paintings of this period, between 1500 and 1501 (plates 100, 101, 111–113). This masterpiece, now in London (plate 114), is dense with religious and moral meanings but retains a perfect limpidity. If the *Calumny* betrayed, despite its great style, some didactic overtones, here the idiom remains absolutely lyric. We would only point to the handling of space, a talent that was only Botticelli's, recalling the drawings for the *Divine Comedy*. The sense of a third dimension is not missing, but the steep incline of the roof of the stable, with the accents of the rocks on either side against the background of dark trees, tends to force the spatial movement toward a single plane. The color makes an exquisite pattern of blues and golds, against the green of the forest, and scintillating yellow of the thatched roof. This panel which has so many primitive qualities about it that do not deny the artistic progress of the Renaissance but contrast it with an intense nostalgia for the Middle Ages, was painted just when Leonardo was working on the second cartoon (now lost) for his *St Anne*. We can agree with Argan that the work has a marvelously archaic spirit through which Botticelli was arguing against the scientific naturalism and secularism of Leonardo. For him beauty was a moral truth, and could be attained only through faith. In fact, his faith was such that—as Ruskin intuited—he was potentially a religious reformer.

After this conclusive masterpiece, Botticelli's activity decreased. His solitary art probably no longer satisfied the public. The makers of taste and mores were by then turning to the young and new artists. The others, the traditionalists, went to his *bottega* for the tondos of *Madonnas* and altarpieces of *Redeemers* that had the traditional and popular piety quite different from the deep spiritual sense of the master. In 1503, one of Isabella Gonzaga's agents found Perugino and Filippino Lippi too busy, and only "Alessandro Botechiella" available and "ready to serve willingly."

But when he painted, he was still able to create works of great spiritual tension. For example, the *Mystic Crucifixion* in the Fogg Museum (plate 119), or the series about St Zenobius (plates 120–125). In this splendid work, a tormented and complex line articulates and divides the groups; the architecture of the backgrounds opens onto forced and improbable perspectives and reveals, beyond the scene of the drama, hallucinating visions of emptiness.

We do not know of any works later than this one, which was probably finished in 1505. Of his last years, there is no trace. We can imagine his spirit as being very much alive to the very end, but it remained in meditative solitude. Even official records contain no further word of him until his burial was recorded on May 17, 1510, in the cemetery of the Church of Ognissanti.

From the mythological idylls of the *Primavera* and of the *Birth of Venus* to the mystic enthusiasm of the *Mystic Nativity* and the awed drama impressed in the St Zenobius cycle, it may appear that the trajectory of Botticelli's art hardly followed a logical course. But the unity of his means, that line which includes and summarizes in discreet or open allusions all the values of volume and space, attests to the unity of his vision throughout his long career. Unity of stylistic means signifies the unity of idiom and of inspiration. While the serene quality of his early and mature works was mitigated by a touch of subtle melancholy and dissatisfaction, his late works—no matter how sincere and genuinely felt was the quest of the spirit in them—still projected all the images into a world of legend. Botticelli's inspiration was greatest at the moment when movement becomes stasis, when life becomes memory, when reality becomes image and symbol . . . and history passes over into myth. And here, in infinite varieties of tone, is the most constant lyrical nucleus of his art.

# BIOGRAPHICAL NOTES

1485. Botticelli is painting an altarpiece he began at the beginning of the year or at the end of 1484 for the chapel of Agnolo de' Bardi in the Church of Santo Spirito, now in the Berlin museum (cf. comment on plate 20).

1487. Paints a *tondo* for the audience hall of the Palazzo Vecchio, which is probably identifiable as the *Madonna of the Pomegranate* in the Uffizi.

1488–90. Paints the *Annunciation*, now in the Uffizi, for the Guardi Chapel in the monastery church of Cestello in Borgo Pinti, now named Santa Maria Maddalena de' Pazzi (cf. comment on plate 38). Also the *Coronation of the Virgin* for the chapel of Sant'Alò (Eligius) of the Goldsmiths, in the Church of San Marco (cf. comment on plate 42).

1491. Member of a commission, along with Lorenzo di Credi, Ghirlandaio, Perugino, and Baldovinetti, to judge a competition for the design of the façade of the Duomo, on January 5. On May 18, the Works of the Duomo commission him to decorate in mosaic two sections of the vault in the Chapel of San Zanobi in Santa Maria del Fiore, along with Gherardo and Monte di Giovanni. The other two sections were given to Ghirlandaio and his brother David. On August 25 and December 23, 1491, and again on December 18, 1492, he receives payment for this work, which he leaves incomplete (finished later by David Ghirlandaio).

1493, MARCH 30. His brother Giovanni, the dealer called "Botticello", dies. In the meanwhile, Simone, his younger brother, returns from Naples and goes to live with Sandro.

1494, APRIL 19. Acquires a house and land with his brother Simone outside Porta San Frediano, near Bellosguardo. Luca Pacioli cites Botticelli alongside Filippino Lippi and Ghirlandaio as a "master of perspective" in his book, *Summa de arithmetica geometria, proportione et proportionalità*, published that year in Venice.

1495. From a letter from Lorenzo di Pierfrancesco de' Medici's wife, dated November 25, we learn that Botticelli is expected at their villa in Trebio "to paint certain things for Lorenzo."

1496. From June 14 to August 14, he paints a *St Francis* in the dormitory of the convent of Santa Maria di Monticelli outside Porta San Frediano. Michelangelo addresses a letter "To Sandro di Botticello in Florence" from Rome on July 2, which was intended for Lorenzo di Pierfrancesco de' Medici.

1497. Executes some decorations with the aid of assistants in Lorenzo di Pierfrancesco de' Medici's villa in Castello. On July

2, the estate manager accepts Botticelli's charges in the name of Lorenzo, who had been away from Florence since March.

1498. From a tax declaration, we learn that Sandro lives with his brother Simone, in their nephews' —Benincasa and Lorenzo—house in the Santa Maria Novella quarter. Income from their land is declared as 156 florins. On February 18, he promises in a formally notarized document not to offend the shoemaker Filippo di Domenico del Cavaliere, his neighbor near the villa outside Porta San Frediano. The shoemaker makes a similar statement.

1499. Under November 2 in his diary, his brother Simone writes: "Alessandro di Mariano Filipepi, my brother, one of the good painters our city has these days, in my presence as we sat by the fire about three in the morning, told how on that day in the workshop in his house he had been talking with Doffo Spini about the case of Fra Girolamo (Savonarola). And Sandro asked him in effect to tell him the whole truth, because he knew Doffo had been one of the principals in the affair since they were always examining it. What sins had they found Fra Girolamo had committed, Sandro wanted to know, to deserve such a vile death. And then Doffo answered him, 'Sandro, must I tell you the truth? We never found any, neither mortal nor even venial.' Then Sandro asked him: 'But then why did you make him die such a terrible death?' He answered: 'It wasn't I; the cause was Benozzo Federighi. And if we hadn't condemned this prophet and his followers and had sent them back to St Mark's, the people would have put us in sacks and cut us to pieces. Things had gone too far, and we decided for our own safety that they should die.' Then they said things which are not necessary to repeat."

On November 15, Botticelli joins the Doctors and Apothecaries Guild because the corporation had been reorganized after a period of decadence in its authority over artists.

1501. At the beginning of the year, he finishes the *Mystic Nativity*, as we read from the inscription in Greek on the painting itself (cf. comment on plate 114).

1502. On September 23, Francesco de' Malatesti writes to the duchess of Ferrara, Isabella Gonzaga d'Este, that Perugino, whom she wants to complete the decoration of the study left unfinished by Mantegna, is in Siena and that Filippino Lippi, whom he had also asked, is too busy. He proposes Botticelli: "Another one, Alessandro Botechiella, has been much praised to me as an excellent painter and as a man who works willingly, and he isn't busy like the others. I had someone talk to him and he says . . . he will serve Your Excellency willingly."

On November 16, Botticelli was accused of sodomy, but it appears the case was not pursued. Mesnil observes (1938) that in that period, accusations of sodomy were as frequent as accusations of subversion are among political enemies in our own day.

1503. Ugolino Verino records as famous painters Giotto, Taddeo

Gaddi, Pollaiuolo, Filippino, Domenico and David Ghirlandaio, Leonardo and Botticelli in his poem, *De illustratione urbis Florentiae*.

1503–5. During these years, Botticelli is charged a number of membership fees, as recorded in the books of the Company of St Luke. On October 18, 1505 the account is settled, presumably with the paintings about the life of St Zenobius.

1504. On January 25, he takes part in the commission of artists who were chosen to decide where to place Michelangelo's *David*. Botticelli and Cosimo Rosselli suggest the steps in front of the Duomo.

1510. We learn from the *Book of the Dead* of Florence and from the *Book of the Dead* of the Doctors and Apothecaries Guild that Sandro Botticelli was buried in the cemetery of the Church of Ognissanti on May 17.

# BOTTICELLI'S PAINTINGS

### Color Plate I

MADONNA OF THE MAGNIFICAT.
*Florence, Uffizi.*

### Plate 1

MADONNA OF THE MAGNIFICAT.
*Panel, diameter 118.\* Florence, Uffizi.*
Acquired in 1784 as an anonymous
work from a certain Ottavio Mag-
herini. The attribution to Botticelli
probably goes back to Cavalcaselle
(1864), and is universally accepted.
Milanesi (1878) thought it might be
the *tondo* mentioned by Vasari in San
Francesco (later San Salvatore) al
Monte, in Florence, which Bocchi
also spoke of (1591). But Vasari had
specified eight angels while this
painting has five; the only Botticelli
*tondo* with eight angels is the *Raczinsky Madonna* in Berlin (see Part I,
plate 63). The painting has faded as a
result of earlier cleanings and is quite
changed, especially the faces of the
Virgin and Child, by overpainting
which tends to "sweeten" the expressions more than necessary.
Cavalcaselle thought it a very youthful effort and noted Lippi's marked
influence. Ulmann (1893) decided it
was later, around 1482, or after the
Roman visit. Horne (1908), A.
Venturi (1925), Gamba (1936) and
Argan (1956) agree, while Yashiro
and later Van Marle place it around
1481, before his departure for Rome,
around the time he painted the *San
Martino Annunciation*. Bode, on the
other hand, along with Schmarsow,

L. Venturi and Bettini, thinks it later
than the *Madonna of the Pomegranate*,
which he dates around 1482, and
places it around 1485. Mesnil is not
so exact, but he does speak first of
the *Madonna* in Berlin (plate 20)
which is dated around 1485.

An accurate judgment is difficult
because of the painting's condition.
Taking into account the Roman
"fullness" of the figures, and the
quality of the line, which becomes
more subtle, for instance, in the
*Venus and Mars* (plate 8), I would
tend to place it around 1482–83.
Workshop copies: one in the Louvre
and another formerly in the Morgan
Collection in New York (both lack-
ing the angel who is placing the
crown at the extreme left), probably
identical with the one once in the
Alessandri house in Florence (Ulmann). Yashiro cites a third, located
in some Swiss museum, which is
allegedly divided into two octagons.

### Plate 2

MADONNA OF THE MAGNIFICAT.
Detail: angels at the left.

### Plate 3

MADONNA OF THE MAGNIFICAT.
Detail: the Virgin's head.

### Plate 4

MADONNA OF THE MAGNIFICAT.
Detail: the Virgin's hand and that of
an angel.

\* All dimensions are in centimeters.

## Plate 5

MADONNA OF THE BOOK. *Panel,
58 × 39·5. Milan, Poldi-Pezzoli
Museum.* Origins not ascertained. It
appeared for the first time as a
Botticelli in the catalog of the
museum prepared by Bertini (1881).
Restored and rid of the overpainting
in 1951 (Pellicioli). It has been considered autograph since at least
Morelli (1890) on, except for the
temporary attribution by Venturi to
the artist's school. Generally placed
close to the *Madonna of the Magnificat*
(plate 1), it has been variously dated
between 1481 and 1485, or with
more latitude by Russoli, who puts
1480–90 forward as possible dates. I
prefer dating it with the *Madonna of
the Magnificat*, that is, around 1482–83.

## Plate 6

MADONNA AND CHILD WITH ST
JOHN THE BAPTIST. *Round panel,
diameter 68. Rome, Lazzaroni Collection.* Acquired by the Collection from
Erich's, the antique dealers about
1925. Published by A. Venturi (1925
and in *Vita Artistica*, 1926) as an
autograph work, the painting was
accepted as such by Van Marle,
Gamba and Bettini. Mesnil thinks it
Botticelli's design but the workshop's
execution. It seems for the most part
the master's. Van Marle dates it
around 1491 and Mesnil around the
period of Savonarola's influence, but
Gamba's and Bettini's dating is more
persuasive, that is, around the time of
the *Madonna of the Magnificat*. There is
a copy in the museum at Montpellier.

## PLATE 7

PORTRAIT OF A YOUTH. *Panel,
37·5 × 28·2. London, National
Gallery.* This belonged, it appears, to
Robert Udny, who sold it in 1804
with an attribution to Giorgione. In
1837, it was in the Northwick

Collection for certain, where Waagen
saw it and attributed it to Filippino,
but later to Masaccio. In 1857, it was
put on exhibition in Manchester as a
self-portrait by Masaccio, and the
National Gallery acquired it as such
in 1859. Cavalcaselle proposed the
name of Botticelli with reservations,
but Richter and Frizzoni were more
positive. Ulmann rejected the attribution in 1893 and Bode in 1921
because of the straight-front pose,
the impudent look and the uniform
blackness of the background. After
Horne (1908), however, the attribution has been universally accepted.
Horne thought it might have been
painted in 1482, immediately after
Botticelli's return from Rome, and A.
Venturi and Yashiro agreed (later
changing his mind to 1483), along
with Van Marle and Bettini. Mesnil
did not express an opinion, but
Gamba prefers to date it around the
time of the *Coronation of the Virgin* in
the Uffizi (plate 42); that is, around
1490. But the similarity among the
angels' faces Gamba points out is
more psychological than stylistic,
while the confident design and formal
completeness of the work which
reflect a greater ease than we find in
the portraits in the Sistine Chapel
indicate a date somewhat later, and
close to the *Magnificat*.

## Plate 8

MARS AND VENUS. *Panel, 69 ×
173·5. London, National Gallery.*
Purchased in Florence by Sir
Alexander Barker after 1864, it
passed to the National Gallery in
1871 as a Botticelli. It had been
frequently repainted, but was cleaned
in 1943. Gombrich thinks the wasps
circling about Mars's head are
symbolic of the Vespucci ("little
wasps" in Italian) family. If this is so,
the painting could very well be one
of the "many paintings framed in

decorated walnut used for borders and benchbacks with many lively and beautiful figures" painted by Botticelli "around a room . . . in the Via de' Servi, the Vespucci house" (Vasari). The house, in any case, had been acquired by Vespucci in 1495; since the painting is obviously earlier it could have been moved from another house. But the hypothesis is improbable because according to Vasari the figures were small, and he was probably referring to the *Tragedy of Virginia* and the *Tragedy of Lucretia* (plates 102–103), which, besides, were executed later, easily around 1499. The attribution to Botticelli is universally accepted.

As for the date of execution, Bode and Van Marle consider it around the time of the *Primavera*, date it 1476–78 and relate it to the idyll of Giuliano de' Medici and Simonetta. Schmarsow and later Argan (for different reasons) date it around 1475. Schmarsow thinks it is a headboard that Lorenzo gave to Giuliano on the occasion of the joust. But Ulmann and Horne, as well as the majority of the critics (Yashiro, the Venturis, Gamba, Mesnil, Bettini, Davies) tend to consider it 1485–86 more likely, near the *Birth of Venus* and the frescoes from the Lemmi Villa now in the Louvre (but cf. for the dating of the frescoes my comments on plates 116–117 in Part 2). I would prefer to date it a year or so earlier, around 1483, because the line has not attained that subtle and graceful inflection it achieves in the *Birth of Venus*, while the painting as a whole develops with the same tranquil harmony which characterizes the *Madonna of the Magnificat*. We should reject the romantic explanations which insist on seeing Giuliano and Simonetta in the two figures. The literary source for the painting has not

been identified for certain, despite some relationships with a passage from Lucretius and a passage from the *Stanze per la Giostra* by Poliziano, where, it is true, Mars is asleep, but on Venus's knees. Palm attempted to identify it with a hymn to Venus and Mars composed by Lorenzo the Magnificent. Wickhoff alluded to the short poem by Resposianus (3rd C.), *De concubitu Martis et Veneris*, which contains the episode of Cupid gathering the arms of Mars (but there are several fauns in the painting). Horne pointed out similar themes in paintings by Jacopo del Sellaio and Piero di Cosimo and preferred therefore to consider the theme a tradition of the atelier.

The neo-Platonic interpretation of the allegory proposed by N. N. Robb seems well founded (*Neo-Platonism in the Italian Renaissance*, n.d.) as well as Gombrich's. Here then we have the allegory of Venus understood as Humanity (like Primavera), who has beneficent power over Mars, the symbol of discord and war. The allegory is explained by astrological analogies by Ficino (*Commentario sul Simposio*, v, 8a). Wind offers a similar theory, describing Venus as the symbol of love and harmony who subjugates Mars, the symbol of hate and discord, according to Pico della Mirandola's "harmony of opposites" "and if Mars were to be placed under Venus's sway, that is, the opposite of the principles making up their characters, nothing would ever be corrupted" (*Commento*, II, 6).

## Color Plate II

BIRTH OF VENUS. Detail of plates 12–13.

## Plate 9

MARS AND VENUS. Detail: a satyr and Mars.

Plate 10

MARS AND VENUS. Detail: Venus and the satyr with the helmet.

Plate 11

MARS AND VENUS. Detail: the figure of Venus.

Plates 12–13

BIRTH OF VENUS. *Canvas, 172·5 × 278·5. Florence, Uffizi.* According to the *Anonimo Gaddiano* Botticelli "painted several pictures in the house of Sire Giovanni de' Medici (of the Bande Nere) at Castello, which are among the most beautiful works he has done." Even Vasari cites this painting in the villa at Castello ("Venus being born and those breezes and winds which make her come to earth with her loves"), along with *Primavera*. The work is still recorded as being in Castello in the 1558 and 1638 inventories; it passed to the Uffizi from the grand duke's possessions in 1815. The fact that the painting came from Castello shows, as Horne justly points out, that it was not executed for Lorenzo the Magnificent, but for Lorenzo and Giovanni di Pierfrancesco, for whom the villa at Castello was purchased. Later the villa became the property of Giovanni delle Bande Nere and then Cosimo I. While authorship is certain, and proved by excellent sources and the quality of the painting itself, the date of execution is problematical. Bode considers it stylistically related to the *Primavera*, dating it around 1478, but Schmarsow dates it earlier since he connects it with Giuliano and Simonetta (claiming that Venus is arriving at Portovenere, where Simonetta Vespucci lived). Most scholars date it around 1485 or 1486 —Ulmann, Horne, Yashiro, A. Venturi, Gamba, L. Venturi, Bettini

and Argan. Yashiro referred it to the time of the *Madonna of the Pomegranate* that is, 1487. Mesnil does not specify but indicates a time later than the *Primavera* (cf. Part 2, plates 64–65). Van Marle considers it with the frescoes in the Sistine Chapel, around 1481–82. Of the two most frequently cited dates, 1478 and 1485–86, the latter is probably closer to the truth, but a slight correction may be in order. The harmonious fullness of the *Madonna of the Magnificat* (plate 1) and of the other works of the period gives way to a finer movement of the line, and here for the first time appears that languor the "feeling of exile" which Pater described as characteristic of Botticelli. Thus the work must be later than 1482–83. But on the other hand, in a work which has many affinities with the *Venus*, the *Madonna* in Berlin (plate 20), dated 1485, the linear flow already begins to stiffen, to harden in rather angular formations. The date of execution of the *Birth of Venus* should fall, then, between the *Madonna of the Magnificat* and the Berlin *Madonna*, around 1484. Although the subject was identified by Vasari, J. Meyer attributed the source to a Homeric hymn published in 1488 from a Florentine manuscript, known most probably by the humanistic circles much earlier. Gaspary called attention to Stanzas 99–103 of the *Giostra* by Poliziano (derived in turn from the Homeric hymn) which describe the famous painting by Apelles. Warburg noticed other elements beside those common to the Homeric hymn (Venus brought to shore by Zephyr and welcomed by the Hours), elements exclusively used by Poliziano (several Winds, not one, the shell and the starry mantle). Further, Botticelli only presents one of the Hours, instead of the three who appear in the Homeric hymn and in Poliziano. This Hour corresponds to the Hour of Spring as Ovid describes her in the *Metamorphoses* (II, 27)—"*Verque novum stabat cinctum florente corona*"—and in the *Fasti* (v, 217)—"*Conveniunt pictis incinctae vestibus Horae.*" The composition was not inspired by a single poem, therefore, but was suggested to the painter by a humanist, perhaps Poliziano himself, who added some touches from Ovid to the imagery of the *Stanze*. Wickhoff's theory is more debatable; he thought the anonymous poem of the second century, *Pervigilium Veneris*, where Venus's arrival in Sicily is celebrated, might have been the source for the painting. Here in fact are some similarities; Hora who places the mantle on Venus, that is, Mount Ibla who is asked to present a cloak of flowers; the rain of flowers, rather vaguely indicated; and the two Zephyrs, male and female. But this depends on a reading of the text, and a rather strange one. Gombrich does not deny the relationship with Poliziano, but adds that a passage from Apuleius about Venus-Isis may have figured in the painting. He points out a passage from Ficino in his commentary on Plato's *Philebus* and a similar one from Pico (his comment on Benivieni's *Canzone d'Amore*, II, 17), both of which interpret Hesiod's account of the birth of Venus. Hesiod tells that Venus was born from the fall of Sky's testicles (he was castrated by Saturn) into the sea, and this is interpreted as the birth of Beauty from the variety and abundance of ideas which come down from God (Saturn) to the mind (Sky) in distorted form. This kind of neo-Platonic interpretation, that is, that Beauty (or Humanity or civilization

according to Ficino's letter) is born from the union of spirit and matter, of idea and nature, seems the more likely to me. More so, that is, than Argan's notion: "humanity is born to civilization, is born from nothing and lands on the shores of nature, who welcomes and dresses her." Even more dubious is Welliver's interpretation that Venus is the symbol of Lorenzo's ideal of the beautiful woman, who in turn is to be identified with the beloved city Florence.

Plate 14

BIRTH OF VENUS. Detail: the Zephyrs.

Plate 15

BIRTH OF VENUS. Detail: the figure of Venus.

Plate 16

BIRTH OF VENUS. Detail of plate 14.

Plate 17

BIRTH OF VENUS. Detail: the figure of the Hour.

Plate 18

BIRTH OF VENUS. Detail of plate 15.

Plate 19

BIRTH OF VENUS. Detail of plate 15.

Plate 20

MADONNA AND ST JOHN THE BAPTIST AND ST JOHN THE EVANGELIST. *Panel, 185 × 180. Berlin, Staatliche Museen.* The *Book* of Antonio Billi (Petrei Ms.) records among Botticelli's works a "panel in Santo Spirito, showing St John." The *Anonimo Gaddiano* specifies that "in Santo Spirito there is a panel of the altar in the Chapel of the Bardi family painted by his own hand, showing our Lady and St John the Baptist." Vasari records it also: "in Santo Spirito in Florence, he made a panel for the Bardi Chapel, which is worked with diligence and well finished, and there are several olive and palm branches done with the greatest love," and leaves, with the other sources, no doubt about its identity. It was transferred to the Bardi house certainly before 1677, the date of the first edition of Cinelli's *Bellezze di Fiorenza*, which records a painting by Vignali in its place. It was then sold, according to Vasari's commentators (Le Monnier edition, 1846), to an antique dealer in 1825, and then to Rumohr, who bought it for the Berlin museum, in 1829. We have no information about the predella which unquestionably completed it. Supino published (1899) documents showing that it was painted between the beginning of 1485 (or the end of 1484) and August, 1485. The documents record a payment to Giuliano da Sangallo for the frame, now lost and a payment in August, 1485 to Botticelli for the painting.

### Plate 21

MADONNA AND ST JOHN THE BAPTIST AND ST JOHN THE EVANGELIST. Detail: the Virgin and Child.

### Plate 22

MADONNA AND ST JOHN THE BAPTIST AND ST JOHN THE EVANGELIST. Detail: John the Baptist with the Virgin and Child.

### Plate 23

ST JOHN THE BAPTIST. *Drawing, 36 × 15·5. Florence, Uffizi.* The traditional attribution to Botticelli is generally accepted. The drawing has been variously related in time to the *St Augustine* in Ognissanti (around 1481), to the *St Barnabas Altarpiece* (plate 29) and to the *Coronation of the Virgin* in the Uffizi (plate 42), that is, around 1490, to the period immediately following his Roman stay, to the *Trinity* in the Lee of Fareham Collection (Part 2, plate 130), around 1477–78. It corresponds stylistically to the altarpiece formerly in Santo Spirito in Florence and now in Berlin (plate 20), which has been dated 1485.

### Plate 24

PORTRAIT OF A YOUTH. *Panel, 45·5 × 31. Washington, D.C., National Gallery of Art.* This once belonged to the Pourtalés and Shickler Collections in Paris, where it was attributed to Masaccio. It then was acquired by the Hamilton Collection in New York and later by the Clarence Mackay Collection in Roslyn, Long Island, New York. Berenson is responsible for the attribution to Botticelli, which almost everyone accepts, except R. Fry and Mesnil. Berenson's statement that the painting dates to Botticelli's mature phase, just before the crisis over Savonarola, which Valentiner agreed with (*Catalog of the Mackay Collection*, 1926) is defined more closely as 1482–85 by A. Venturi; Yashiro; *Duveen Pictures*; Bettini. At times we read 1488–90: Van Marle and Gamba. L. Venturi (*Pitture italiane in America*, 1931) dates it back to the 1470s. Typological and stylistic affinities with the *Madonna of the Pomegranate* (plate 25) make a date around 1487 more probable. The rather sentimental rendering impairs the expressive consistency of the form, so that we cite Bettini's reservations rather than Berenson's praises:

"... a little more than a picture, if not of plagiary of his own work than of distraction."

## Plate 25

MADONNA OF THE POME-GRANATE. *Round panel, diameter 143·5. Florence, Uffizi.* Described as a Botticelli in the inventory of the works in Cardinal de' Medici's collection in 1675, the painting went to the Uffizi from the grand duke's possessions in 1780. Horne proposed that it was the same *tondo* Milanesi described, a *tondo* Botticelli allegedly painted for the audience hall in the Palazzo Vecchio. But Milanesi forgot to cite his sources. The original frame, decorated with a frieze of lilies, seems to confirm that the painting was done for a public office. Bettini, A. Venturi and Gamba accept Horne's identification. Other scholars, both before and after Horne's proposal, suggested other dates, without taking into account the information Horne had used. Thus Ulmann (1893) puts it before 1480, but after the *Raczinsky Tondo* (cf. Part 2, plate 63), but Bode, Schmarsow, Yashiro and L. Venturi place it after the Roman visit, around 1482. Van Marle insists it was done before the Roman visit, around, that is, 1480–81, close to the *Madonna of the Magnificat* (plate 1). Neither Berenson nor Mesnil accept 1487, and the latter thinks the painting quite later than the *Madonna of the Magnificat*, which he dates around 1485. To identify the painting with the *tondo* executed in 1487 may be uncertain, but the style certainly lends itself to that period.

## Plate 26

MADONNA OF THE POME-GRANATE. Detail: the Child.

## Plate 27

MADONNA OF THE POME-GRANATE. Detail: the hands of the Child and of the Virgin with the pomegranate.

## Plate 28

MADONNA AND CHILD WITH ST JOHN THE BAPTIST. *Fragment of a panel, 46 × 41. Edinburgh, National Gallery of Scotland.* Formerly in the Fuller Maitland Collection. A. Venturi published it as an autograph Botticelli, near in time to the *Madonna of the Pomegranate* and the *Birth of Venus* in his book *Grandi Artisti Italiani*, 1924, and in *Botticelli*, 1925. Berenson thinks it authentic, but Van Marle, Gamba and Mesnil consider it a workshop product. I think it substantially autograph, and it should be dated a little after the *Madonna of the Pomegranate*, that is, around 1488.

## Plate 29

ST BARNABAS ALTARPIECE. *Panel, 268 × 280. Florence, Uffizi.* Showing the Virgin enthroned with the Child, four angels and SS Catherine of Alexandria, Augustine, Barnabas, John the Baptist, Ignatius, Michael the Archangel. The first mention is made by Albertini in 1510 ("... in St Barnabas' there is a large panel by the hand of Sandro Botticelli), later confirmed by the *Book* of Antonio Billi ("... in St Barnabas, the panel of the high altar of Our Lady and St Catherine ...") and more briefly by Vasari. The painting was enlarged, at the top and bottom, by Agostino Veracini in 1717, according to Richa's report. In 1808, when the convent was suppressed, it was transferred to the Accademia, and then in 1919 it was taken to the Uffizi, where the additions were removed. While no one has ever doubted Botticelli's authorship because of the authority of the sources, the dating remains controversial. Ulmann proposes the earliest date, around 1480, and Van Marle the latest, around 1494. Between these extremes, most scholars prefer to date it closer to the Roman stay, that is, around 1482–83. Gamba, followed by Bettini and Argan, thinks it was begun about 1487 and continued over several years. Even Mesnil considers it later than the *Madonna* in Berlin (plate 20), which was done around 1485. The close affinities, especially in the Virgin and Child, with the *Madonna of the Pomegranate* (1487) on the one hand, and with the *Annunciation* and the *Coronation* in the Uffizi (1489–90) on the other (plates 38 and 42), leave no doubt that the altarpiece should be dated around 1488. The analogies in the composition and in the type of throne with Filippino Lippi's *Altarpiece of the Eight* (Uffizi), done in 1485, should not lead one to date the Botticelli work earlier, since Botticelli's style in 1485 is demonstrated by the *Madonna* in Berlin as being somewhat different and earlier than the style we find here. Nor should we insist on always saying that it was Filippino who was inspired by Botticelli, especially since in this altarpiece the latter was faced for the first time with a *pala* of considerable size. We publish an old photograph which shows Veracini's additions, because when these were eliminated (obviously the panel had been cut before Veracini enlarged it), the painting became disproportionate.

### Plate 30

ST BARNABAS ALTARPIECE. Detail: Madonna and Child.

### Plate 31

ST BARNABAS ALTARPIECE. Detail: St Barnabas.

### Plate 32

ST BARNABAS ALTARPIECE. Detail: St John the Baptist.

### Color Plate III

ST BARNABAS ALTARPIECE. Detail of plate 29.

### Plate 33

ST BARNABAS ALTARPIECE. Detail: hand of St Michael the Archangel.

### Plate 34

ST AUGUSTINE. *Panel, 20 × 38. Florence, Uffizi.* This and the works reproduced in plates 35–37 are the four surviving pieces of the seven (one for each of the saints with Christ in the center) which formed the predella of the *St Barnabas Altarpiece* (plate 29) and which were separated in 1717. Cavalcaselle considered them to be workshop products, but the majority of scholars consider them, for the most part, autograph. We are faced with splendid paintings, not only in their conception, but also in their execution, despite some unusual touches which anticipate future developments. The theme of this section is taken from the *Golden Legend* and other hagiographic writings. St Augustine is meditating on the shore about the Holy Trinity, when a child appears, intent on filling a small hole with sea water. When the saint asked him what he was doing, the boy answered that he was going to pour the ocean into the hole. The saint protested that the task was impossible, and the boy answered: "It will be easier for me to succeed in pouring the entire sea into this small hole than for you to succeed in making the immense mystery of the Trinity enter your small intellect."

## Plate 35

PIETÀ. *Panel, 21 × 41. Florence, Uffizi.* We can discern tiny figures and the climb to Calvary in the landscape. (See comment on plate 34.)

## Plate 36

SALOME. *Panel, 21 × 40·5. Florence, Uffizi* . (See comment on plate 34.)

## Plate 37

EXTRACTION OF THE HEART OF BISHOP IGNATIUS. *Panel, 21 × 38. Florence, Uffizi.* Once attributed to Ghirlandaio, as evidenced by the writing on the back, which describes the scene as an episode from the life of St Augustine. Later it was believed to refer to St Ambrose. Horne was the first to show that the saint was Ignatius, referred to in the *Catalogus Sanctorum* by Pietro de' Natali, the bishop of Aquileia, and in other hagiographic sources. The episode was taken as a sacred subject set in Florence. St Ignatius is being tortured on Trajan's orders, but continues to invoke Christ's name. His persecutors asked him why he cried out that name, and he answered that it was written on his heart. When he died, his heart was removed and the name of Christ was found stamped on it in gold. (See comment on plate 34.)

## Plate 38

ANNUNCIATION. *Panel, 150 × 156. Florence, Uffizi.* This was found in 1870 in a chapel in the Palazzetto Villa in the San Martino a Terenzano quarter (Fiesole), which had belonged to the nuns of St Mary Magdalene de' Pazzi in Borgo Pinto since 1744. The Uffizi acquired it in 1872. Thus we have evidence that it came from the Church of St Mary Magdalene de' Pazzi, which belonged to the Cistercian monks in the fifteenth century. Vasari's note seems, therefore, to refer to this painting: "at the monks' in Cestello, (Botticelli) did an *Annunciation* in a chapel . . ." Milanesi found an interesting notice in the *Book of the Benefactors of the Monastery of Cestello in Pinti*, begun in 1480: "on March 19, 1488 (1489 by modern calendars) Benedetto di Ser Giovanni Guardi had a chapel built in Cestello in Florence, the second on the right upon entering, called the Chapel of the Annunciate . . . expenses for my work, that is, for me Don Antonio for masonry in said chapel (were) fifty ducats . . . and the other expenses in said chapel (were) for the panel by the hand of Sandro Botticelli . . ." (cf. also *Dell'antica chiesa dei Cistercensi, oggi S. M. Maddalena de' Pazzi*, 1881; C. de Fabriczy, in *L'Arte*, 1906; Horne, 1908). We learn that the chapel was consecrated in 1490. The painting is therefore documented and dated; Botticelli painted it between 1489 and 1490. Ulmann, Bode, L. Venturi, and Mesnil consider it autograph. Morelli, Yashiro, Van Marle, Berenson, Gamba and Bettini think it a workshop product. Everyone agrees, however, that the drawing is the master's, as well as much of the actual execution. Bettini attributes the reddish and opaque coloring to Filippino Lippi. A fine workshop rendering is the *Pietas Christi* at the foot of the Cross.

## Plate 39

ANNUNCIATION. Detail: the landscape.

## Plate 40

ANNUNCIATION. Detail: the angel.

Plate 41

ANNUNCIATION. Detail: the Annunciate Virgin.

Plate 42

CORONATION OF THE VIRGIN. *Panel, 378 × 258. Florence, Uffizi.* Originally in the Church of San Marco, in the Chapel of Sant'Alò, where it is recorded by a number of sources: Albertini (1510), the *Book* of Antonio Billi (Petrei Ms.), the *Anonimo Gaddiano* and by Vasari (1550 and 1568). In 1596, it was replaced by a *Transfiguration* by G. B. Paggi (Richa) and taken to the chapter where Rosselli's *Sepultuario* records it in 1657. In 1807 it was taken to the Accademia in Florence, and in 1919 to the Uffizi. Variously dated, once as around 1480 (Ulmann), or as around 1500, the painting was definitely dated by some documents Mesnil (1903) and Horne (1908) discovered as being between 1488 and 1490. This is made clear from a *List of Obligations and Masses*, 1525, in which we read that the Goldsmiths Guild appropriated a fund in 1488 in order to have the Office of the Dead said in the Chapel of Sant'Alò in the Church of San Marco in the month of December, and that "the said Guild, besides this, ordered the panel." The date 1490 is suggested by another document which confirms that the chapel was in use by then. Critics agree that assistants helped paint the robes of the saints (John, the Evangelist, Augustine, Ambrose and Eligius).

Plate 43

CORONATION OF THE VIRGIN. Detail: the head of St Augustine.

Plate 44

CORONATION OF THE VIRGIN. Detail: the angelic choir, at the left.

Color Plate IV

ANNUNCIATION. Detail of plate 38.

Plate 45

CORONATION OF THE VIRGIN. Detail: the angelic choir, at the right.

Plates 46a–48

PREDELLA OF THE CORONATION OF THE VIRGIN

The predella is made up of only one panel (21 × 269) and is also kept in the Uffizi in Florence. A work of very high quality, comparable only to the upper part of the main panel, it is so well done that only a few (Mesnil and Bettini) have been able to detect an assistant's hand in the rather Filippino-like coloring. There are five tales in all: *St John on Patmos* (plate 46a); *St Augustine* (plate 46b); *Annunciation* (plate 47a); *St Jerome* (plate 47b); and the *Miracle of St Eligius* (plate 48). In the last episode, St Eligius, the protector of goldsmiths, reattaches a woman's nose and a horse's hoof in his farrier's shop.

Plate 49

CORONATION OF THE VIRGIN, WITH FOUR SAINTS. *Canvas, 100 × 178. New York, Julian Bache Collection.* The saints are Anthony Abbot, John the Baptist, Julian and Francis. In chronological order, it passed from the Burne-Jones Collection in London to the Cassirer in Berlin to the Von Lichnowski in Austria. Beside being published in the Bache catalog (1929), it was published by A. L. Mayer (*Pantheon*, 1930), by Wortham (*Apollo*, 1930), by Cortissoz (*Magazine of Art*, 1930), with dates ranging from 1495 to 1500. Van Marle considers it as around 1490–95; Berenson, before 1486. The chronology proposed by Gamba and

Bettini is more likely; that is, close to or soon after the *Coronation of the Virgin* in the Uffizi (plate 42). There is a comparison, in fact, in the tension and impulse of the line, between the predella and this panel (plates 46a–48).

### Plate 50

ANGEL. *Drawing, 9·2 × 9·5. Bologna, private collection.* Bertini published it in 1953 at the suggestion of Arcangeli and Garritt. Rightly dated close to the *Coronation of the Virgin*, formerly in San Marco in Florence and now in the Uffizi (plate 42). Around 1490.

### Plate 51

ANGEL. *Drawing, 27 × 18. Florence, Uffizi.* Pen, watercolor and white lead highlights. The traditional attribution is generally accepted, but Popham had doubts (1931). Yashiro thinks it was done around 1483–84; Van Marle, around 1485–90; Berenson relates it to the *St Barnabas Altarpiece* (plate 29) or with the *Madonna of the Book* in Milan (plate 5); Gamba considers it earlier than this *Madonna*, and Bertini justifiably dates it near the *Coronation* in the Uffizi (plate 42), that is, around 1490.

### Plate 52

MADONNA AND CHILD WITH ST JOHN THE BAPTIST. *Panel, 89·5 × 73·5. Dresden, Gemäldegalerie.* Although considered autograph by Morelli, Jähnig, and Gamba, it is frequently cited among the workshop products (Ulmann, A. Venturi, Van Marle, Berenson, Mesnil) or passed over. Only Jähnig considers it a late work, while Gamba puts it close to the *Calumny* (plates 92–93). But it appears closer to about 1490. The theme echoes a youthful work in the Louvre (Part 1, plate 8), but with the pathos and anxiety characteristic of this period. Various versions of the *bottega*, without St John, can be found in London, Frankfurt and in Milan (the Crespi Collection, formerly belonging to the Prince of Lichtenstein).

### Plate 53

MADONNA AND CHILD WITH ST JOHN. *Round panel, diameter 84. Williamstown, Clark Museum.* Once in the Triquetti Collection in Paris, then from 1886 to 1951 (Charpentier sale, December 10) in the Nolleva Collection. It has been unpublished until now, but it is justifiably attributed to Botticelli, dated around 1490, by Longhi and Gamba in letters to the owners. Of very high quality and unquestionably autograph.

### Plate 54

MADONNA OF THE PAVILION. *Round panel, diameter 65. Milan, Ambrosiana.* The origins have not been ascertained, but the attribution to Botticelli is traditional. Horne, and later Gamba, assume that this is the painting Vasari mentions— ". . . the small *tondo* by his (Sandro's) hand which can be seen in the room of the prior of the Angels' in Florence, with small figures, but very pretty and carefully done." The place is the Monastery of Santa Maria degli Angeli in Via degli Alfani, which was suppressed in 1808. Apart from Ulmann's opinion that related it in time to the *Madonna of the Magnificat* (plate 1), critics generally agree in assigning it to the period just after 1490. The drawing has the same impulse which animates the robes of the angels in the *Coronation* in the Uffizi (plate 42).

### Plate 55

MADONNA OF THE PAVILION. Detail: the Virgin.

## Plate 56

ANNUNCIATION. *Panel, 24 × 36. New York, Lehman Collection.* Before this reached the Lehman Collection, it was in the Barberini Gallery in Rome, and then in the Huldschinsky Collection in Berlin. Morelli judged it a school product, followed by Horne and A. Venturi, but it is considered autograph by Ulmann, who dates it close to the *St Barnabas Altarpiece*, but he dates this latter painting later than 1480; by Bode, with a date around 1485–90; by Yashiro, with a date around 1474; by Gamba, dating it just before the *Calumny* (plates 92–93), that is around 1495. Mesnil does not comment on it, and neither do Bettini and Argan. The high quality leaves no doubt as to its being autograph, and the vibrant linearity of the angel brings it close to the *Madonna of the Pavilion* (plate 54).

## Plate 57

PALLAS. *Drawing, 19 × 6·6. Milan, Ambrosiana (Resta Ms., folio 14).* Pen. Once attributed to Filippo Lippi, it was then attributed to Botticelli by Berenson, followed by Yashiro, Van Marle, Gamba and Bertini, with a date rightly put after 1490, close to the *Madonna* in the Ambrosiana (plate 54).

## Plate 58

PALLAS. *Drawing, 22 × 14. Florence, Uffizi.* Black pencil, pen, highlights in white lead on prepared rose paper. Horne recognized it in 1908 as a drawing for the tapestry executed in Flanders for Count Guy de Baudreuil, still in Viscount de Baudreuil's possession in Favelles, Loire-et-Cher (cf. Müntz, *Histoire de l'art pendant la Renaissance*, I, 1889; and Des Forts, in *Congrès Archéologique de France*, 1905). Since Guy de Baudreuil became abbot of St Martin-aux-Bois in 1491, and the tapestry shows an abbot's mitre, the drawing he ordered from Florence must be after that date (cf. also, concerning the design for a medal of Francesco Laurana, Wittkower, in the *Journal of the Warburg and Courtauld Institutes*, 1938–39). Traditionally ascribed to Botticelli, it is ascribed to the *bottega* by Horne and Berenson. More correctly, however, Yashiro, Van Marle, Gamba, Bertini consider it autograph and date it later than 1491 except for Yashiro, who dates it around 1483–84. Deriving from this drawing is the analogous drawing by the workshop now at Oxford, which Gamba mistakenly insists is autograph.

## Plate 59

ST AUGUSTINE IN HIS CELL. *Panel, 41 × 27. Florence, Uffizi.* Vasari notes it in the house of Bernardo Vecchietti as a work by Filippo Lippi. In the eighteenth century, it belonged to the Ignatius Hugford Collection, and in 1763, it was put on exhibition as a Fra Filippo during a showing of old paintings held by the Academicians of Drawing in the second cloister of the Annunziata in Florence. Piero Pieralli acquired it and sold it to the Uffizi in 1779, still attributed to Lippi. Morelli attributed it to Botticelli in 1877. Horne explains the continuous attribution to Lippi as deriving from Vasari's claim, and that the painting was known as a Botticelli when it was in Vecchietti's possession. In fact, Borghini remembered a "beautiful painting at Vecchietti's" (1584), but does not mention any paintings by Lippi. The Botticelli catalogs universally include it, and the dating is variously put at around 1490 (Ulmann, Horne, Bode, Van Marle, Mesnil); around 1495

(Bode, 1921; A Venturi, Gamba); about 1500 (Yashiro and Bettini). The evident relationships in the plastic consistency of the drawing and in the chiaroscuro with the *St Barnabas Altarpiece* (plate 29) and with the *Coronation* in the Uffizi (plate 42) lead us to date it close to 1490.

Plate 60

MADONNA AND CHILD. *Round panel, diameter 60. Washington, D.C., National Gallery of Art (Kress Collection)*. Formerly in the Parvey Collection in Paris, it then was acquired by the Wildenstein in Paris in 1929, and soon after taken to the United States. A. L. Mayer first published it as a Botticelli, with a date around 1490 (in *Pantheon*, 1930), and the attribution was accepted by Van Marle, who dated it around 1490–91, and by L. Venturi, who dated it around 1481. Although ignored by the other critics, it appears to be quite fine and vibrating with a subtle lyricism. We should date it around the time of the *Madonna of the Pavilion* (plate 54).

# LOCATION OF PAINTINGS

AMSTERDAM

VON RATH COLLECTION
*Judith* (plate 101).

BARCELONA

CAMBÓ COLLECTION
*Portrait of Marullus* (plate 62).

BERGAMO

ACCADEMIA CARRARA
*The Tragedy of Virginia* (plates 102, 104, 106).
*Savior* (plate 154; attribution).

BERLIN

STAATLICHE MUSEEN
*Madonna and St John the Baptist and St John Evangelist* (plates 20–22).
*Drawings for the Divine Comedy* (plates 78–80).
*Portrait of a Young Woman* (plate 128; attribution).
*Venus* (plate 131a; attribution).

BOLOGNA

PRIVATE COLLECTION
*Angel*, drawing (plate 50).

BOSTON

ISABELLA STEWART GARDNER MUSEUM
*The Tragedy of Lucretia* (plates 103, 107–110).
*Nativity* (plate 140; attribution).
MUSEUM OF FINE ARTS
*Madonna and Child with St John the Baptist* (plate 142; attribution).

BRUSSELS

BAUTIER COLLECTION
*Lamentation* (plate 150; attribution).

CAMBRIDGE

FITZWILLIAM MUSEUM
*Adoration of the Magi*, fragments (plates 71b–73).
FOGG ART MUSEUM
*Mystic Crucifixion* (plate 119).
*Savior* (attribution).

CINCINNATI

EDWARDS COLLECTION
*Madonna and Child with St John and an Angel* (plate 133b; attribution).

DARMSTADT

KUPFERSTICHKABINETT
*The Faithless and the Descent of the Holy Ghost*, drawing (plate 99).

DRESDEN

GEMÄLDEGALERIE
*Madonna and Child with St John the Baptist* (plate 52).
*Miracles of St Zenobius* (plate 125).

EDINBURGH

NATIONAL GALLERY OF SCOTLAND
*Madonna and Child with St John the Baptist* (plate 28).

# FLORENCE

CORSINI GALLERY
*Madonna and Child with Angels*
(plate 146b; attribution).
PITTI PALACE
*Madonna and Child with St John the Baptist* (plate 63).
UFFIZI GALLERY
*Madonna of the Magnificat* (plates 1–4).
*Birth of Venus* (plates 12–19).
*St John the Baptist*, drawing (plate 23).
*Madonna of the Pomegranate* (plates 25–27).
*St Barnabas Altarpiece* (plates 29–33).
*Vision of St Augustine*, predella (plate 34).
*Pietà*, predella (plate 35).
*Salome*, predella (plate 36).
*Extraction of the Heart of St Ignatius*, predella (plate 37).
*Annunciation* (plates 38–41).
*Coronation of the Virgin* (plates 42–45).
*St John on Patmos*, predella (plate 46a).
*St Augustine*, predella (plate 46b).
*Annunciation*, predella (plate 47a).
*St Jerome*, predella (plate 47b).
*The Miracle of St Eligius*, predella (plate 48).
*Angel*, drawing (plate 51).
*Pallas*, drawing (plate 58).
*St Augustine in His Cell* (plate 59).
*Nativity*, drawing (plate 64).
*(Unfinished) Adoration of the Magi* (plates 70–71a).
*Faun*, drawing (plate 88).
*Calumny* (plates 92–98).
*St Jerome*, drawing (plate 157; attribution).
*Study for a Saint*, drawing (attribution).

# FRANKFURT

STÄDELSCHES KUNSTINSTI-TUT

*Portrait of a Young Woman* (plate 127; attribution).

# GLASGOW

ART GALLERY AND MUSEUM
*Annunciation* (plate 113).

# GRANADA

CAPILLA DE LOS REYES
*Agony in the Garden* (plate 112).

# GREENVILLE (SOUTH CAROLINA)

BOB JONES UNIVERSITY
*Pentecost* (plate 148; attribution).

# HAMBURG

KUNSTHALLE
*Nude Youth*, drawing (plate 90).

# HANOVER

NIEDERSÄCHSISCHE LANDESGALERIE
*Annunciation* (plate 100).

# LONDON

BRITISH MUSEUM
*Faith*, drawing (plate 91).
NATIONAL GALLERY
*Portrait of a Youth* (plate 7).
*Mars and Venus* (plates 8–11).
*Mystic Nativity* (plates 114–118).
*Vocation of St Zenobius* (plates 120–121).
*Miracles of St Zenobius* (plates 122–123).
*Portrait of a Young Woman* (plate 130a; attribution).
*Angel*, reverse side of above (plate 130b; attribution).
*Madonna and Child with St John the Baptist* (plate 139; attribution).
*Madonna and Child* (plate 145a; attribution).
*Madonna and Child with St John the Baptist* (plate 146a; attribution).

# MILAN

### AMBROSIANA
*Madonna of the Pavilion* (plates 54–55).
*Pallas*, drawing (plate 57).
*St Thomas*, drawing (plate 68).
### POLDI-PEZZOLI MUSEUM
*Madonna of the Book* (plate 5).
*Pietà* (plates 66–67).
*Coronation of the Virgin* (plate 159; attribution).

# MONTELUPO (FLORENCE)

### CHURCH OF SAN GIOVANNI
*Madonna and Child with Four Saints*, predella (attribution).

# MUNICH

### ALTE PINAKOTHEK
*Pietà* (plate 65).

# NEW YORK

### BACHE COLLECTION
*Coronation of the Virgin, with Four Saints* (plate 49).
### DUVEEN COLLECTION
*Tondo of the Madonna and Child with St John* (plate 155a; attribution).
*Madonna and Child* (plate 156; attribution).
### KNOEDLER GALLERIES
*Spring* (plate 137a; attribution).
*Summer* (plate 137b; attribution).
*Autumn* (plate 138a; attribution).
*Winter* (plate 138b; attribution).
### LEHMAN COLLECTION
*Annunciation* (plate 56).
### METROPOLITAN MUSEUM OF ART
*The Last Communion of St Jerome* (plate 69).
*Miracles of St Zenobius* (plates 124, 126).
### PIERPONT MORGAN LIBRARY
*Fragment of the Adoration of the Magi* (plate 72).

### ROCKEFELLER COLLECTION
*Madonna and Child with St John the Baptist* (plate 141; attribution).

# OTTAWA

### NATIONAL GALLERY OF CANADA
*Jesus and St John the Baptist* (plate 134a; attribution).

# PARIS

### LOUVRE
*Miracle of St John the Evangelist* (plate 111).
*Portrait of a Boy* (plate 134b; attribution).
### MUSÉE JACQUEMART-ANDRÉ
*Flight Into Egypt* (plate 153; attribution).

# PHILADELPHIA

### MUSEUM OF ART
*Portrait of Lorenzo Lorenzano* (plate 61).

# ROME

### BORGHESE GALLERY
*Madonna and Child with St John and Angels* (plate 144; attribution).
### COLONNA GALLERY
*Madonna and Child* (plate 145b; attribution).
### LAZZARONI COLLECTION
*Madonna and Child with St John the Baptist* (plate 6).
*Portrait of a Man* (attribution).
### PALLAVICINI COLLECTION
*The Derelitta* (plate 89).
*Transfiguration with St Ambrose and St Augustine* (plate 147; attribution).

# TURIN

### GALLERIA SABAUDA
*Venus* (plate 132; attribution).

## VATICAN CITY

VATICAN ART GALLERY
*St Sebastian* (plate 149; attribution).
VATICAN LIBRARY
*Drawings for the Divine Comedy*
(plates 74–76).

## VIENNA

AKADEMIE DER KUNST
*Madonna and Child with Angels* (plate
143; attribution).

## WASHINGTON, D.C.

NATIONAL GALLERY OF ART
*Portrait of a Youth* (plate 24).
*Madonna and Child* (plate 60).
*Madonna Enthroned* (plate 151a;
attribution).

## WILLIAMSTOWN
(MASSACHUSETTS)

CLARK MUSEUM
*Madonna and Child with St John*
(plate 53).

## LOCATION UNKNOWN

*Drawings for the Divine Comedy*,
formerly in Berlin, Kupferstich-
kabinett (plates 77, 81–86).
*Portrait of Dante*, formerly in Hat-
field, Burns Collection (plate 87).
*Portrait of a Young Woman*,
formerly in Munich, Darnheim
Antiques (plate 129a; attribution).
*Portrait of a Young Woman*, formerly
in Richmond, Cook Collection
(plate 129b; attribution).
*Venus*, formerly in Lucerne (plate
131b; attribution).
*Madonna and Child*, formerly in
Berlin, Simon Collection (plate
133a; attribution).
*Madonna of the Candles*, formerly in
Berlin, Kaiser Friedrich Museum
(plate 135; attribution).
*Annunciation*, formerly in Berlin,
Kaiser Friedrich Museum (plate
136; attribution).
*Madonna and Child*, formerly in
Paris, Trotti House (plate 151b,
attribution).
*Annunciation*, formerly in Florence,
Corsini Gallery (plate 152a; attri-
bution).
*Annunciate Virgin*, formerly in
Florence, Corsini Gallery (plate
152b; attribution).
*Baptism of Christ*, formerly in
Faenea, Guidi Collection (plate
155b; attribution).
*Annunciate Angel*, formerly in
Leningrad, Hermitage (plate 158a;
attribution).
*Annunciate Virgin*, formerly in
Leningrad, Hermitage (plate 158b;
attribution).
*Madonna and Child*, formerly in
London, Benson Collection (attri-
bution).
*Madonna and Child with St Joseph*,
formerly in Berlin, Simon Collec-
tion (attribution).
*Madonna and Child with St John*,
formerly in Vienna, Lanckoronsky
Collection (attribution).
*Madonna and Child with St John*,
formerly in Paris, Dreyfus Collec-
tion (attribution).
*Noli me tangere* and *Resurrection*, cited
by Van Marle (attribution).
*Christ Crowned with Thorns*, for-
merly in Paris, Lazzaroni Collec-
tion (attribution).
*The Young Redeemer*, formerly in
New York, Kleinberger Galleries
(attribution).
*St Dominick*, formerly in Lenin-
grad, Hermitage (attribution).
*St Jerome*, formerly in Leningrad,
Hermitage (attribution).

# REPRODUCTIONS

# ACKNOWLEDGEMENT FOR
PLATES

*B. Anderson, Rome:* plates 1-3, 5, 15-18, 29, 34-38, 42, 44, 45, 54, 59, 63, 89, 102, 129b, 139, 144-45b, 154. *Mansell-Anderson:* plate 25. *Alinari, Florence:* plates 21, 30, 46, 47, 52, 70, 127, 146b. *Gabinetto Fotografico della Sovrintendenza a'le Gallerie, Florence:* plates 12-13, 23, 51, 58, 64, 71a, 88, 92-98, 157. *Brogi, Florence:* plates 4, 14, 19, 26, 27, 31-33, 39-41, 43, 55, 152. *National Gallery, London:* plates 7-11, 114-18, 120-23, 130, 146a. *Bildarchiv Foto, Marburg:* plates 20, 22, 143. *National Gallery of Art, Washington:* plates 24, 60, 151a. *Claudio Emmer, Milan:* plates 48, 66, 67. *Metropolitan Museum of Art, New York:* plates 49, 69, 124, 126. *Walter Scansaini, Milan:* plates 57, 68. *Stearn and Sons Ltd, Cambridge:* plates 71b, 73. *Archivi Vaticani:* plates 75, 149. *Gardner Museum, Boston:* plates 103-10 and 140. *Walter Steinkopf, Berlin-Dahlem:* plates 128, 131a. *Staatliche Museen, Berlin:* plates 135, 136. *Knoedler Galleries, New York:* plates 137, 138. *Duveen Brothers, New York:* plates 155a, 156. *Annan, Glasgow:* plate 28. *Clark Museum, Williamstown:* plate 53. *Lehman Collection, New York:* plate 56. *Johnson Art Collection, Philadelphia:* plate 61. *F. Serrra, Barcelona:* plate 62. *Bayerische Staatgemälde-sammlungen, Monaco:* plate 65. *Pierpont Morgan Library, New York:* plate 72. *Kleinhempel Fotowerk-satten, Hamburg:* plate 90. *British Museum, London:* plate 91. *Niedersächsische, Landesgalerie, Hanover:* plate 100. *A y R. Mas, Barcelona:* plate 112. *Art Gallery and Museum, Glasgow:* plate 113. *Fogg Art Museum, Cambridge, Mass.:* plate 119. *Deutsche Fotothek, Dresden:* plate 125. *Art Museum, Cincinnati:* plate 133b. *National Gallery of Canada, Ottawa:* plate 134a. *Archives Photographiques des Monuments Histori-ques de France, Paris:* plate 134b. *Museum of Fine Arts, Boston:* plate 142. *Bob Jones University, Greenville:* plate 148. *Bulloz, Paris:* plate 153. *Museo Poldi-Pezzoli, Milan:* plate 159. *National Gallery, London:* color plate IV (Part 4). Material for the remaining color plates was supplied by *Scala, Florence.*

MADONNA OF THE MAGNIFICAT
Uffizi, Florence

Plate 1. MADONNA OF THE MAGNIFICAT
Florence, Uffizi

Plate 2. *Detail of plate 1*

Plate 3. *Detail of plate 1*

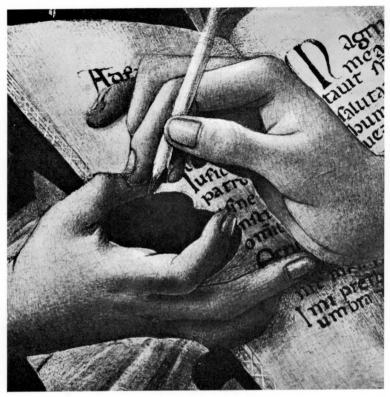

Plate 4. *Detail of plate 1*

Plate 5. MADONNA OF THE BOOK
Milan, Poldi-Pezzoli Museum

Plate 6. MADONNA AND CHILD WITH ST JOHN THE BAPTIST ·
Rome, Lazzaroni Collection

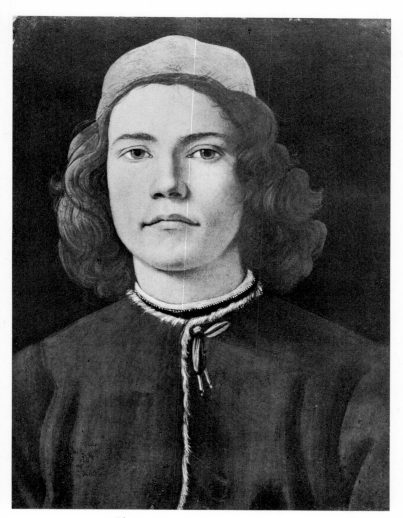

Plate 7. PORTRAIT OF A YOUTH
London, National Gallery

Plate 8. MARS AND VENUS
London, National Gallery

BIRTH OF VENUS
Uffizi, Florence
(*detail of plates 12–13*)

Plate 9. *Detail of plate 8*

Plate 10. *Detail of plate 8*

Plate 11. *Detail of plate 8*

Plates 12-13.
Flor

Plate 14. *Detail of plates 12–13*

Plate 15. *Detail of plates 12–13*

Plate 16. *Detail of plates 12–13*

Plate 17. *Detail of plates 12–13*

Plate 18. *Detail of plates 12–13*

Plate 19. *Detail of plates 12–13*

Plate 20. MADONNA WITH ST JOHN THE BAPTIST AND
ST JOHN EVANGELIST
Berlin, Staatliche Museen

Plate 21. *Detail of plate 20*

Plate 22. *Detail of plate 20*

Plate 23. ST JOHN THE BAPTIST
Florence, Uffizi

Plate 24. PORTRAIT OF A YOUTH
Washington, D.C., National Gallery of Art

Plate 25. MADONNA OF THE POMEGRANATE
Florence, Uffizi

*Plate 26. Detail of plate 25*

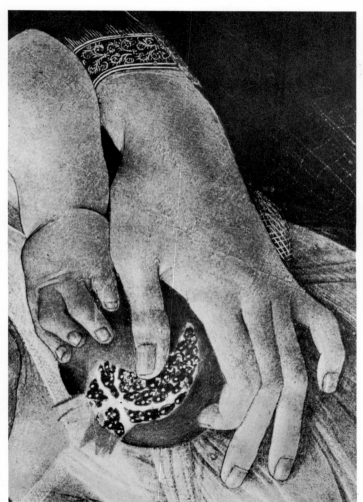

Plate 27. *Detail of plate 25*

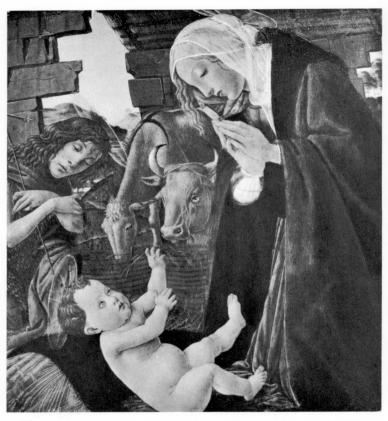

Plate 28. MADONNA AND CHILD WITH ST JOHN THE BAPTIST
Edinburgh, National Gallery of Scotland

Plate 29. ST BARNABAS ALTARPIECE
Florence, Uffizi

Plate 30. *Detail of plate 29*

Plate 31. *Detail of plate 29*

Plate 32. *Detail of plate 29*

ST BARNABAS ALTARPIECE
Uffizi, Florence
*(detail of plate 29)*

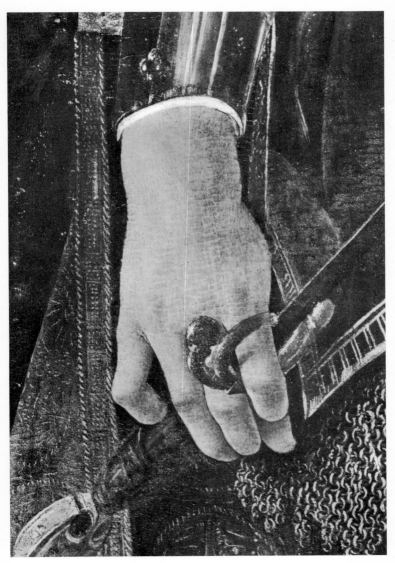

Plate 33. *Detail of plate 29*

Plate 34. ST AUGUSTINE
Florence, Uffizi

Plate 35. PIETÀ
Florence, Uffizi

Plate 36. SALOME
Florence, Uffizi

Plate 37. EXTRACTION OF THE HEART OF BISHOP IGNATIUS
Florence, Uffizi

Plate 38. ANNUNCIATION
Florence, Uffizi

Plate 39. *Detail of plate 38*

Plate 40. *Detail of plate 38*

Plate 41. *Detail of plate 38*

Plate 42. CORONATION OF THE VIRGIN
Florence, Uffizi

Plate 43. *Detail of plate 42*

Plate 44. *Detail of plate 42*

ANNUNCIATION
Uffizi, Florence
(*detail of plate 38*)

Plate 45. *Detail of plate 42*

Plate 46. ST JOHN ON PATMOS and ST AUGUSTINE
Florence, Uffizi

Plate 47. ANNUNCIATION and ST JEROME
Florence, Uffizi

Plate 48. MIRACLE OF ST ELIGIUS
Florence, Uffizi

Plate 49. CORONATION OF THE VIRGIN, WITH FOUR SAINTS
New York, Julian Bache Collection

Plate 50. ANGEL
Bologna, Private Collection

Plate 51. ANGEL
Florence, Uffizi

Plate 52. MADONNA AND CHILD WITH ST JOHN THE BAPTIST
Dresden, Gemäldegalerie

Plate 53. MADONNA AND CHILD WITH ST JOHN
Williamstown, Clark Museum

Plate 54. MADONNA OF THE PAVILION
Milan, Ambrosiana

Plate 55. *Detail of plate 54*

Plate 56. ANNUNCIATION
New York, Lehman Collection

Plate 57. PALLAS
Milan, Ambrosiana

Plate 58. PALLAS
Florence, Uffizi

Plate 59. ST AUGUSTINE IN HIS CELL
Florence, Uffizi

Plate 60. MADONNA AND CHILD
Washington, D.C., National Gallery of Art (Kress Collection)